FROM
PARADISE
LOST
TO
PARADISE
GAINED

From Abandonment to Hope

Joyce Etrata Wachsmuth

WESTBOW
PRESS®
A DIVISION OF THOMAS NELSON
& ZONDERVAN

WestBow Press books may be ordered through booksellers or by contacting:

WestBow Press
A Division of Thomas Nelson & Zondervan
1663 Liberty Drive
Bloomington, IN 47403
www.westbowpress.com
844-714-3454

ISBN: 978-1-6642-3773-5 (sc)
ISBN: 978-1-6642-3774-2 (e)

Library of Congress Control Number: 2021912588

Print information available on the last page.

WestBow Press rev. date: 06/30/2021

To my beloved mom and dad

To my husband, Douglas Alan Wachsmuth

To our children and grandchildren:

    Ted and Stephanie Wachsmuthh (Caleb and Chloe)

    Keoni and Michelle Wachsmuth (Kai, Hana, and Kaleo)

    Beth and Jon Teran (Malia, JD [Joseph Douglas] Kiana)

To my sisters:

    Evelyn Gomera

    Rita Taylor

    Carole Brown

    Mona Estell

To my brothers:

    Sidney Etrata (deceased February 17, 2003)

    Dale Etrata

CONTENTS

Introduction ix

1. Mildred Fernandez 1
2. Here Comes the Judge! 5
3. Life in the Orphanage 9
4. "I have no mother!" 13
5. "You're my mother!" 17
6. A Disturbing Pause in the Story 21
7. Abandoned Again 25
8. Life in Ookala Influenced My Life Today 29
9. Her Story Affects My Story 41
10. My Daddy 47
11. "I Disown You" 51
12. Legacy of My Mom and Dad 55
13. My Spiritual Journey Became Our Spiritual Journey 61
14. The Chain Was Broken 65

Appendix 71

INTRODUCTION

FOR MANY, HAWAII IS A PICTURE OF PARADISE WITH PALM trees and beautiful beaches … a place to just lay in the sun and get a tan. My mom grew up in Hawaii, but her life did not begin with those beautiful images. She was abandoned when she was three; she was taken away from her home, placed in a foster home for a few days, and then went before a judge and was sent to the Salvation Army Home for Girls in Hilo, Hawaii. That experience left a mark on her life—wounds that were hard to erase and many times not visible to others. She began with paradise lost.

My dad, Bonifacio Soriano Etrata (Bonciong), nicknamed Bonzo, grew up in the Philippines. When he was a teenager, he came to Hawaii with his father, Claro Etrata. The two worked on a sugarcane plantation in the 1930s; many Filipinos did that. Initially, they were hired on contract by the Hawaiian government's Board of Immigration. When Hawaii became the territory of the United States in 1900, plantation owners there hired men from the Philippines under Hawaiian Sugar Planters' Association contracts.

The story was that Claro was a gambler who came to Hawaii to earn enough to pay off his debts. When it was time for my dad to go back to the Philippines with him, my dad refused to go, so his father said, "I disown you!" His father abandoned him. My dad never spoke to or saw his father again.

Though my parents had been abandoned, paradise lost ultimately became paradise gained for them. They were resilient. Their stories affected my life, and writing their stories gave me an opportunity to see them as God's story and for His glory. "He heals the brokenhearted and binds up their wounds" (Psalm 147:3 NIV).

I started writing my mom's story many years ago so my children and grandchildren and future generations would know her story. I tried to write her story while she was alive because I wanted her to participate in the process with me, but she died suddenly of a heart attack in 2002. I felt abandoned because I had been looking forward to having more time with her and learning more about her story. Years have passed; I picked up the project from time to time, but the urgency is upon me to finish this book.

I was planning on writing only my mom's story because she had been abandoned as a child. I felt that hers was a unique story of loss and abandonment that ultimately resulted in blessings. But the more I wrote about her story, the more I realized it was about my dad as well. They affected the lives of others in significant ways toward healing, reconciliation, and redemption. My mom would have been 100 years old on December 22, 2021 and my dad would have been 109 on July 24, 2021!

Special thanks to my beloved husband, Doug, who endured the years of my talking about writing the book and being my cheerleader and encourager to finish it. I am truly grateful for his perseverance and patience.

Special thanks to my grandson Caleb, who helped me with my computer needs. I am also grateful for my granddaughter Chloe, who helped with the typing of some of the family history.

I also acknowledge my brother Dale and sister-in-law, Aina, for the use of their work on the genealogy of our family and the story of our dad.

First, let's begin this journey with my mom's story. Why was she abandoned? What happened?

My mother and father

CHAPTER 1

MILDRED FERNANDEZ

M Y MOTHER, MILDRED, WAS BORN IN PAAUHAU, HAWAII, on December 22, 1921. She was called Little Minnie after her mother, Minnie Kamakawiwoole, but she hated being called that.

Paauhau is a little community about fifty miles north of Hilo and about the same distance from Kona on the island of Hawaii. She had thought her birthday was December 23, and we celebrated it on that date, but she later found her birth certificate and learned she had been born the day before that. I was with her when she discovered the correct date and witnessed her disappointment and shock.

Minnie's father—my mom's grandfather—was Charles Kamakawiwoole, a circuit-riding preacher on the island of Hawaii. We were told that it took him two weeks to complete his journey around the island on horseback. He preached the message of Jesus Christ in his Hawaiian language. I know very little about him and Daisy, my great-grandmother, so I'm not sure how he became a

Christian. Their families could have taken part in the great revival in Hawaii; it was recorded that the largest revival west of the Mississippi took place from 1830 to 1860 in Hawaii. There are records that he went to seminary in Kohala, Hawaii, but there are no documents to prove that. (See the appendix for more information on his career as a preacher and his wife, Daisy)

The parsonage my great-grandfather and great-grandmother lived in was next to the church in Paauhau, Hawaii. Today, it is a historical landmark. (See picture in appendix.) I'm not sure if they raised all fifteen of their children there, but I was told that they had some chickens and a garden with bananas, guavas, mountain apple, and lots of vegetables.

Minnie, my grandmother, was the second youngest of the fifteen children and the youngest of the girls. Not sure what she was like as a child. Was she spoiled by her mom and dad and the rest of the siblings because they were a lot older than she was? Was she strong willed? I don't know if her parents were strict and had great expectations for their children. I can only assume that as parents, they expected their children to succeed and live honorable lives walking with the Lord.

With a garden and the large property surrounding the church, my great-grandfather needed help, so he hired a gardener, Jose Villanueva Fernandez, who became my grandfather. I don't know how long he worked as a gardener, but he became acquainted with Minnie. How did they meet? Was their attraction mutual? What did she see in him? Did my grandmother, a teenager then, flirt with him? I can only surmise.

I never spent much time with Jose, my grandfather, but he was very friendly and had a big smile with lots of gold teeth; he was a good-looking man! I don't know when or why he came from the Philippines (Cebu) to work on a sugar plantation. Were my great-grandparents concerned about Minnie's and Jose's relationship? She was seventeen then and he was twenty-two. Maybe they tried to convince my grandmother that this relationship was not good, or maybe they didn't know about it at all. But their relationship grew close, and my grandmother got pregnant.

According to my great aunt Mariah, Minnie was shunned by her father when he found out the news; he felt that she was a disgrace to the family. Her older brothers and sisters were educated as lawyers and teachers, and some were involved in politics. He was probably embarrassed and didn't want anyone to know about her pregnancy. I don't know how Minnie handled the rejection; did she become bitter and resent her parents? I am a grandmother of eight, and I cannot imagine turning my back on any of them no matter the circumstances.

I think my grandmother felt that her only alternative was to elope; they were married on October 21, 1921 in Hilo, when she was seven months pregnant, and my mother was born on December 22, 1921 in Paauhau. I can only speculate that they stayed in Paauhau until my mom was born.

CHAPTER 2

HERE COMES THE JUDGE!

A FTER MY MOM WAS BORN IN 1921, MY GRANDMOTHER AND grandfather moved to Ookala, a community of a few hundred people. They had another child, Robert Fernandez, who was born in 1923. They separated shortly after Robert was born. What were the circumstances of their separation? Not sure, but I can only speculate on the insecurity of my mom, who was so young then. Was she confused when my grandfather moved out? Had she been close to him? My mom could not remember much about when she lived in Ookala, but from my recollection, she loved her father. I visited him in Hilo, but he died when I was in third grade, so I have little memory of him.

Ookala was a small community twenty-three miles north of Hilo. It was really a village made of homes that were clustered together in what were called camps. In the beginning, camps were organized by different ethnic backgrounds such as the Chinese camp, the Japanese camp, and the Filipino camp, but in time, they became more integrated. People there worked either in the sugarcane fields or at the sugar mill. Life was simple but hard.

Why did my grandmother decide to live in Ookala after she separated from my grandfather? Did she have a job? Had Jose found a job in Ookala? They did separate, and my grandmother had to raise two children; she must have found that hard. She might have worked in the cane fields for ten cents an hour, the pay at that time; she had to make a living somehow. At age nineteen or twenty, she might not have been sure that she wanted to take care of her children by herself; she could have felt overwhelmed by her responsibilities.

When my mom was three, someone—maybe a neighbor— reported that she was being neglected. Did someone see her being abused by my grandmother, or was she neglected by being left alone? I tried to picture my mom going from house to house during the day because her mother had gone to work. Maybe my grandmother did ask the neighbors to look after my mom, but perhaps they felt taken advantage of by my grandmother. Someone might have complained to her that her daughter was unsupervised, but I think my grandmother felt she didn't have a choice. One way or another, as it was told by my mother, a police officer came with someone from social services to remove her from her home.

"Where are they taking me?" she cried. "Let me go! I want my mommy!" she screamed when the social worker took her hand. My mom remembered crying as she was taken in a police car to a foster home. She didn't remember where she was taken or what the home was like, but she was so afraid that she refused to talk to anyone. She remembered feeling scared and lonely and crying herself to sleep.

After a few days in a foster home, she was then taken to court. She remembered a stern judge banging his desk with a gavel and saying, "You will be sent to the Salvation Army Home for Girls in Hilo."

My mom shared this story many times with tears in her eyes. She was frightened and kept asking, "Where am I? When can I go back home and see my mommy?" She remembered being very confused when she was being escorted by the social worker, but she was too scared to talk to anyone. She remembered driving for quite a while trying to listen to the conversation going on in the front seat, but nothing made sense. She remembered being very hungry but feeling sick at the same time. "What's going to happen to me?" she cried softly. Finally, they reached a building, and a woman walked my mom up the stairs. The matron said, "This is your home now."

LIFE IN THE ORPHANAGE

MY MOM REMEMBERED BEING TAKEN TO A ROOM IN THE basement of the Salvation Army Home for Girls in Hilo. "I was so scared because the girls I saw looked so much older than me, and I felt so small," she said. "They put me on a bed that had only springs and some newspaper. I wondered if the foster parents I had been with had told them that I had wet the bed at night."

A matron told her that she would get a mattress when she no longer wet her bed. She wasn't sure how long that took her, but it took a while. She said that she was so ashamed and embarrassed when they had to change her. She remembered the room being really dark with just one lightbulb hanging on a cord from the ceiling. She cried herself to sleep every night many times trembling.

She remembered being afraid of the older girls because they were tall and spoke in very harsh tones when they told her, "You need to wake up now and get dressed!" and such. They had been abandoned by their families and were in pain themselves. My mom was so relieved when they moved her upstairs with the rest of the girls, but she was still afraid.

"I cried myself to sleep every night," she said many times. "I kept praying, 'Please help me, God. When I grow up, I want a happy home.'" She was mistreated by the older girls, whom she feared. She would receive extra food and treats if she did their chores for them.

Her experiences there made her decide to never mistreat the younger girls who came into the orphanage after her. She remembered making sure that the younger girls were taken care of because many of them came into the orphanage frightened and many times very hungry. She made sure that they were not taken advantage of and would sneak food to them.

My mom had a lot of compassion for those who were in need of food and shelter. When we were growing up, she had us share our clothes with those in the community who needed them. My mom taught us to take care of those less fortunate than us. Along with my sisters we would iron the clothes and put them in bags to give to those who needed them in our community.

In the orphanage, she was very serious about learning about God; that gave her hope and comfort. She loved knowing that God was going to take care of her and that she was not alone. (Jeremiah 29:11NIV) reads, "'For I know the plans I have for you,' declares the Lord, 'plans to prosper you and not to harm you; plans to give you hope and a future.'" God brought comfort and hope to her life.

She shared how she had asked Jesus into her heart when she was five. She felt that the Lord looked after her throughout her life. She was very proud when she was given a Bible; she memorized Psalm

91. (When she died, the one thing I wanted was her Bible, and it was wonderful to have my brothers and sisters grant that request.)

She started kindergarten when she was five. She would walk to school with the rest of the girls; there were thirteen of them. As a group, they were very noticeable because they wore hand-me-down clothes. Other children made fun of them and treated them as outcasts, but they supported each other and made sure they walked together to and from school, about a quarter of a mile.

Life felt safe in the orphanage, but it was also hard. She felt lonely a lot of the time, but she hid her feelings by being a good student at school and obeying the matrons.

She persisted asking the matrons, "When will my mother come to get me?" But the days turned to months and the months turned to years, and she finally resolved, "I have no mother!"

CHAPTER 4

"I HAVE NO MOTHER!"

FOR ELEVEN YEARS, HER MOTHER NEVER VISITED HER. SHE was tempted to go to the office and see her records to find out where she had come from. They kept reassuring my mom that someday she would meet her mom, and she said that she prayed every night for that, but she said, "Eventually, I stopped praying."

My mom made up her mind to be a good student and maybe one day become a matron at the home. The matrons there were very strict, but my mother warmed their hearts. She obeyed them and did well in school. The home was very disciplined; the girls were expected to do their chores quickly and with a good attitude. My mother had us do our chores with a good attitude because we were part of the family. She considered it very important that we learned how to cook, clean the house, and be hospitable to any guests. It was also important to her that we ate together as a family. I have a lot of wonderful memories of those meals.

We were not allowed to disrespect our brothers and sisters; we were taught to love each other. We didn't want her to find out when we disagreed with each other because the older of the two quarreling would be reprimanded. To this day, I have a hard time disagreeing with my brother and sisters. At all costs, we want peace, love, and harmony with each other.

From a very early age, my mom decided she wanted to go to college. She mentioned how the matrons encouraged her to do well in school so she could receive a scholarship. She was an intelligent and conscientious student. She went to grade school at Kapiolani School in Hilo and Hilo Intermediate for junior high along with other girls from the home, but she felt labeled and isolated from the rest of her schoolmates; her dresses were clean but ragged, and she felt ashamed about that. But it did not stop her from doing her best and being at the top of her class. She was looking forward to going to college and succeeding there.

In her later years, my mother's aunt, Aunty Mariah, told her stories about my grandmother. My mom had a lot of questions about her family. I had the privilege of being with my mom at Aunty Mariah's home when I was in high school. Aunty Mariah was a beautiful Hawaiian woman who wore a beautiful hibiscus flower in her hair. She was married to a very sweet Japanese man named Mr. Tanaka. I wish I had paid better attention because my mom found her conversations with her aunt very enlightening; she kept saying, "Oh! Now I know that happened!"

My mom remembers walking on Kilauea Street, where a woman with long, white hair would greet her and the twelve other girls from the home. She would give them all cookies, but she would give my mom an extra hug and a kiss and would cry. For years, my mother wondered why the woman would speak words of endearment in Hawaiian to her. Aunty Mariah told my mom that the woman who had given her the extra hugs was her grandmother, Anna Daisy Kamakawiwoole. Her grandmother would keep looking around to see if anyone was watching her. My aunty said that Anna Daisy must have known that my mother was living at the home and did not want her husband, my mom's grandfather, Charles Kamakawiwoole, to know that she was hugging her grandchild. If my mom had only known that the woman was her grandmother. What special reunion that would have been for my mom and her grandmother!

Now that I am the grandmother of eight beautiful grandchildren, I can't imagine not being able to embrace and enjoy them. To know that my mom had been sent to a home for girls is beyond my comprehension. I have a lot of questions about my grandmother's behavior because she did not make any attempt to find out where her daughter had been taken.

I don't have any stories about my grandfather Jose Fernandez knowing about my mom being in the Salvation Army Home. I don't think he knew where my mother was until she came out of the home at age fifteen. The sad thing is that the Salvation Army Home was so close to where my grandfather lived. Had he tried to find her, or had he thought his ex-wife was taking care of her? He had a gentle smile and a kind heart; he would give each of us a quarter every time we visited him. So many questions have gone unanswered because he died unexpectedly of a heart attack when he was fifty-seven, when I was in third grade.

CHAPTER 5

"YOU'RE MY MOTHER!"

WHEN MY MOTHER WAS FOURTEEN, SHE WAS CALLED into the matron's office and was told that she did have a mother and that she was in the office waiting to take her home. My mom took one look at the woman sitting in the office and cried, "I have no mother, and I have no home!" She ran out of the office. She cried uncontrollably and was very angry; she wondered why her mother had waited so long to get her out of the home. She had given up hope that she had a mother or a father.

She dreamed and fantasized about living in a happy home with a mother and father. She wanted to be in a loving home so badly that whenever she saw a family with a mom and a dad, she cried. She had decided that she was going to college and would become a Salvation Army matron so she could help girls who had also been abandoned.

She thought after the first visit that it would be the last time she would see her mother, but her mother came several times over the months trying to take her home, but my mom refused to go. My mom wondered what had changed my grandmother's mind about her. No one knows; she might have felt guilty for having abandoned her. My grandmother had four children after my mom. Did she need a babysitter? My mom, a fourteen-year-old, would have filled that need.

My mom wanted to believe that this was her mother. She shared that she wanted to go with her but was scared. Her mother came with gifts such as beautiful dresses and a purse enticing her to go home with her.

Finally, on one of the visits and after refusing for several times to go with her "claimed" mother, she sat there crying. As she looked at her mother's toes (her mother was wearing flip-flops; in Hawaii, we call them slipas), she remembered her mother's toes from when she was three. Her big toe had a distinct look, and she cried, "You are my mother! I remember your toes!" She embraced her mom like she had never done before. "You are my mother!" she said over and over.

My mother, age fifteen then, was scared and excited about leaving the home and living with her mother, but to know that she had a mother felt good. She remembered saying goodbye to her friends at the home. She felt bad that they had to stay there.

She remembered being very scared when her mother drove her to her home. Her mother seemed friendly but very stern. Along the way, she realized that she had never been to the places they were passing. She remembered seeing plants all the same and later realized that they were sugarcane. The roads were very bumpy, unlike those in Hilo; she was going to the country.

She felt awkward meeting her two brothers—Robert, age twelve, and Alfred, age eight, and her sister, Nora, age ten. She was disappointed that she wasn't able to go to school because it was far away. She told my grandmother, "I want to go to school. I want to attend college!" Her mother refused to answer her, and eventually, my mom quit asking.

She was grateful to be in a home, but she felt she didn't belong. She saw how my grandmother favored her other children, not her, but she would tell herself that at least she was in a home, not an orphanage. She stayed busy helping with the chores and tried not to complain about anything for fear that she would be sent back to the home. She missed her friends, but she enjoyed the freedom of being in a home and being able to play at the park.

She enjoyed going to community parties and baseball games there. It was at one of those games that she met my dad, and at one of the community parties, my dad kept serving her food. My mom was very shy, but my dad pursued her. My parents didn't talk much about their courtship, but they shared about meeting each other at parties and how my dad had noticed her. I loved hearing them share about meeting each other and how they liked each other.

CHAPTER 6

A DISTURBING PAUSE IN THE STORY

M Y MOM HAD A HARD TIME TALKING ABOUT WHAT IT WAS like to go home with her mother to a place with a tin roof, no washing machine, her mother gone a lot, and babysitting the children. *Was I brought home to take care and babysit children? What about going to school? Will I be able to go to college?* She had many questions. She felt once again abandoned, forced to do chores, and having to live with a mother who had not wanted her from the beginning!

After only a few days of living with her mother, she wanted to return to the Salvation Army home. She missed her friends, and she missed the structure there. Ookala, where my grandmother lived, was twenty-three miles from Hilo. At the time, there was no train between where she was and Hilo; she had no escape.

Her mother was not the sweet and kind person she had seemed

to be when they had met at the home; she realized that this would be a pause in her story in that it was different from being in the Salvation Army home.

When my siblings and I were children, we wondered if our mom had been abused physically and maybe sexually. She mentioned that when she met my dad when she was fifteen, she considered him a very nice and kind man, which made us think that possibly the men she had met through my grandmother were not. Did she become a sex slave? She wanted to get away from my grandmother's home, and she saw the way out—to get married. My dad was ten years older than her, and my grandmother made it clear that she was not happy with my mom marrying my dad. My grandmother thought that she was going to lose her babysitter, house cleaner, and cook! Being with her brothers and sister made her feel that she had a family, but she felt alone all the time.

She told us many times, "I didn't like being in the home, but something happened that I will have to take to my grave." How was she really treated? Was she abused? Did something happen that she was ashamed of?. Had she been forced to have relationships with men? Since she refused to tell us, we could only guess what had happened to her. Though it wasn't her fault, she accepted the blame for whatever it was. One way or another, she was anxious to get out of her mother's home. My siblings and I were sad about whatever had happened to her; we speculated about it because of my grandmother's lifestyle.

My mom's and dad's relationship grew from that first encounter at the park. My mother saw the kindness and gentleness in my father and wanted to marry him; she saw this as a way out of her mother's home. My grandmother treated her differently once she became involved with my dad.

I'm not sure of all the reasons, but my grandmother told my dad that he had to pay her $250 if he wanted to marry my mom. At the time, my dad worked on a sugar plantation, and there was a store where the people in the village could buy groceries on credit. My grandmother bought groceries in my dad's name totaling about $200 and expected him to pay the bill.

She made it very difficult for my mom to be with my dad; they had to sneak around to spend time with each other. Even when the wedding date was decided on, my grandmother tried every way she could to postpone it. Finally, when they were on their way to get married, my grandmother tried to drag my mom out of the car they were driving. My mom was so embarrassed and cried all the way home.

At the wedding, my grandmother apparently interrupted the event, took all their wedding gifts and the money that was given to them, and stopped the reception. My grandmother told the people who came to the wedding to go home. My mom and dad were so embarrassed as some people didn't get a chance to eat and did not know what was going on. One can only imagine what this must have been like for my mom and dad—beginning their married lives with very little money because my grandmother took all their money at the wedding!

CHAPTER 7

ABANDONED AGAIN

ONCE AGAIN, MY MOTHER FELT ABANDONED AND neglected by her mother. My mom was with child by the time they were married. She told us how difficult it was at the beginning, but they survived and persevered by hard work and the support of the community. They had their first child, Evelyn, right away, and my mother remembered how difficult it was for her being a mother at age seventeen.

They lived in Mill Camp, a place where homes were unpainted and constructed cheaply with tin roofs; it had a community bathhouse and outhouse. The individual camps were separated by dirt roads. There were people from Japan, China, Philippines, Korea, and Portugal there; many didn't speak English. My mom said they were friendly and they laughed a lot. Hawaiian Pidgin English originated with the plantation workers trying really hard to communicate with each other, and a new language was born. It was made up of many idioms inserted in mispronounced words; correct grammar was not an issue. I grew up with my siblings and children in my village speaking Hawaiian Pidgin English. I love hearing my family speaking in Pidgin English when I am with them today, and I feel at home whenever I hear people speaking in Pidgin. We spoke Pidgin at school with our friends, but we were encouraged to speak correct English in the classroom. Some teachers didn't care, but other teachers would correct us.

The people communicated by sharing their ethnic foods. The Filipinos made many pork dishes such as pork, peas, and pimientos; many dishes made with fish sauce such as *pinacbet*, chicken papaya, pancit, and chicken or pork adobo, etc. Some Filipino desserts were made from coconut milk, and cascaron were coconut balls made with coconut and mochi flour, deep fried with syrup on the outside. *Bibinca* was made with coconut milk, sweet rice, and brown sugar baked in banana leaves. (Today, I bake it in a 9" x 13" pan.)

Hawaiians added to the menu with kalua pig (pig roasted underground), haupia (coconut dessert made with coconut milk and mochi flour), and laulau (meat and taro leaves wrapped in banana leaves and cooked in a steamer or put underground with the roasted pig). The Japanese shared their teriyaki beef and chicken, ramen noodles (saimin), and sushi. The Chinese shared their chow mein and *manapua* (a steamed bun with char sui meat, barbecued pork, in the middle). The Koreans shared their kalbi beef and kim chi. The Portuguese shared their sweet bread and malasadas (hot donuts).

For many, Hawaii is about the sunshine and warm beaches, but for Hawaiians, it's all about the food! Sharing food was central to growing up in a rural community. There were parties to which the whole community was invited by word of mouth—no formal invitations so no one would be left out. The word spread fast when there was a party. Our phones were on party lines; several neighbors would share one line. You would pick up the phone, and if you heard the dial tone, you made your call, but if someone was using the line, he or she would tell you to hang up. Well, as a child, I found it very tempting to listen to other people's conversations, and I remember being spanked for doing that.

My mom and dad survived by working hard and making sure that their children were loved and protected. In Ookala, people cared for each other and families supported each other. There was an elementary school, a store, a hospital, a post office, and a movie theater, and people went to baseball games and attended parties.

Beyond the social gatherings of the community, there was one Catholic church and a Buddhist gathering place. My dad and mom encouraged us to go to church every Sunday and confession on Saturdays at the Catholic church. There were no protestant church in the community and my dad was Catholic, so my mom joined the Catholic Church. We learned about God, and we were taught that if we did not go to church and did not get a chance to go to the priest for confession, we would go to hell. I lived in fear many times of this consequence, so confession was very important to me. Many times, we had to walk over a mile to meet a priest and confess our sins. I wouldn't say I had a relationship with God but I learned about God and tried to obey. I went to catechism once a week during the school year. There were nuns that came to the school to teach us about God. I remember fondly how kind they were and during my elementary years I aspired to become a nun later in life.

In eighteen years, my mom and dad had seven children: Evelyn, Rita, Carole, Joyce (me), Sidney, Mona, and Dale. My mother prayed that she would have a happy family. From my perspective, she really tried very hard, but life was tough. My dad worked long hours, and I can only imagine all she had to do. I was in the middle of the pack; I helped with chores and took care of my younger siblings. Life was very simple growing up in our small community. We lived in Kukui Village in a very simple home with three bedrooms. I remember making mud pies and playing with my friends in the village in old chicken coops.

Eventually, my parents built a home on the hill in Milo Village with four bedrooms and two bathrooms. We moved in when I was in the third grade. The home had beautiful oak floors, and the contractor who built it added a lot of features that were unique for their time. Our home overlooked the ocean, so we had a beautiful view of whales and ships. I have many fond memories of living there. We had an avocado tree and papaya tree that we loved to climb. My parents had a beautiful garden with anthuriums and orchids. My dad also had a very beautiful vegetable garden. We would call it a self-sustaining garden today.

CHAPTER 8

LIFE IN OOKALA INFLUENCED MY LIFE TODAY

As I mentioned, my parents' first home was in Mill Camp in Ookala, a village with dirt roads, unpainted houses, and rusty tin roofs. The houses, which were very close to each other, were provided by the plantation company. Only some had windows. Chickens and roosters roamed freely and sometimes came into the houses.

As I mentioned, Evelyn was their first; she was born in 1938, Rita was born in 1940, and Carole was born in 1941. Laundry was done by hand in cauldrons hung over a fire; it took all day, but it was a communal affair in that it took place in a community wash house. My dad was working on a sugar plantation for ten cents an hour while my mom took care of the house and children. My mom eventually bought a washing machine, but she would hang her clothes out to dry; she never owned a dryer.

Because she had been abandoned, she was very protective of her children and took them wherever she went. She made friends in her village, and they watched each other's children. They had outhouses that my older siblings remember. One story my older sisters tell is about when my oldest sister decided to see what the outhouse was all about and fell into the hole! Thank goodness she landed on some newspapers and someone heard her crying. (Evelyn, who is now eighty three, hates hearing that story!) They also had one bathhouse for women and one for men. They would heat water over a fire for the wooden tubs.

It was very important to my mom that we had meals together. Even though my dad was not there in the evening, he made time for us during the day even when he should have been sleeping. He loved taking us to the beach whenever he could; he loved to fish, so I remember the fish and *opihis* (small limpids) he caught. He raised chickens and planted a large garden. In our village, my dad won a contest by growing the largest cabbage; he had his picture in the local newspaper, and we were so proud of him!

"Let's sing together while we do the dishes," Rita or Carole would suggest, and without any hesitation, we would start harmonizing in our alto and soprano voices. It made doing the dishes fun! I have many memories of my brothers and sisters singing the popular songs of the day. My brother Sidney and I loved harmonizing "Dream" by the Everly Brothers. My sister Mona and I loved doing dance routines such as "Summer in the City."

My mom always got upset if her children argued with each other; she would correct us and tell us that we were to love each other. She put a high value on harmony in the family. My mom did not accept our voicing our opinions. Because conflict was not tolerated in our home, we siblings would argue away from our mom. Our home was peaceful in many ways, but it was not normal; we didn't learn that it was normal to disagree and voice our opinions as long as it was done respectfully.

She prayed that as a family we would get along and always love each other. Her prayers were truly answered because my brothers and sisters and I respect each other and love spending time with each other. We have had several family reunions at my parents' home in Ookala and Waimea. I can close my eyes and imagine the beautiful times together. We would have a special gathering to kick off the reunion, and we ate, played, sang, and danced together. I can relive those times through video recordings and photographs.

A special time was when each family participated in a talent show—amazing talent! I carried that tradition into my family. Thank you, Mom and Dad, for the many special times we had as a family! Several of reunions were on other islands, and my mom and dad saved up so they could pay for hotels or condos for each family. Because of their generosity, I enjoy doing that for my family too.

My sister Rita lives in Shreveport, Louisiana with her husband Robert, and we talk on the phone almost every day. Mona lives in Denver, and we love to talk on the phone and share our lives. Dale lives in Sacramento, and we stay in close touch by texting and phone calls. They are truly my best friends. We love spending time with each other and have planned several vacations together. We can talk to each other, and we always have time for a good laugh!

Unfortunately, as of this writing, our sister Carole lives on Oahu and is in assisted living in Kapolei. She has Alzheimer's, so time with her is very limited, but it is special. Carole was five years older than me and was very good to me. She included me in everything she did.

We had a lot of fun. Our oldest sister, Evelyn, lives in an assisted living home in Honokaa, Hawaii. We love visiting with her when we can. Carole and Evelyn are gentle souls who lived their lives serving their families and the extended families. Their sons and daughters are now our contact with them, and they are so giving and generous to us as their uncles and aunts.

My brothers and sisters taught me how to love unconditionally, laugh, and enjoy life. My mom passed on the legacy of unity, laughter, and fun. We played a lot of games. She taught us a song that I will never forget. These are the words:

Magdalina, Pagdalina, Leubensteiner, Wallendiner, Hogan, Loga, Pogan was her name.

She went out riding day by day, where she went was hard to say …

Magdalina, Pagdalina, Leubensteiner, Wallendiner, Hogan, Logan, Pogan was her name.

She had some teeth in her mouth; some pointed north and some pointed south.

Magdalina, Pagdalina, Leubensteiner, Wallendiner, Hogan, Logan, Pogan was her name.

She had some hair on her head—half were alive and half were dead.

Welcome
to
Ookala

The Ookala Sugar Co.
Plantation
Est. 1869

Elevation 371

Ookala Village Sign

The Ookala Elementary School (me, second row fifth from the left)

My family in the 1960's (I am next to my dad)

My siblings Mona, Dale, and Sidney

Me and some of my family (Front row: Me, Mona, and
Sidney; Back row: Carole, Evelyn, my mother, and Rita)

We had fun singing this song with our children and grandchildren!

My mother wanted us to sacrifice for one another. We were expected to share with our brothers and sisters no matter what we had. *Kompung*, which means share, was encouraged. We had to give our brothers and sisters a good portion of what we had or the best of what we had. That was difficult for me at times, but it taught me to sacrifice for my brothers and sister.

As I mentioned, we were not a normal family because we had normal disagreements and jealousies but could not show that in front of our mom. She may have felt that if we argued with each other, we would not be the happy family that she dreamed about, and she was fearful of what might happen. I know now that healthy families have disagreements but that they can be resolved in a healthy way.

In Ookala, no one locked their doors. People came to visit without an invitation. People cared for each other and shared whatever they had. We had a large garden, so we shared our vegetables and fruit. I cannot remember anyone being in want of food. My mom did not learn to drive until she was sixty-two and retired. I marvel at how we were able to get anywhere without my mom driving us.

My mom taught her daughters to dance the hula; she was a very graceful hula dancer, and I wanted to dance just like her. Bending your knees helps you dance with grace, but it was so hard to learn that. The song that she taught us to dance was "To You Sweetheart, Aloha." At family reunions, we danced the hula together, so I have many fond memories of dancing the hula with my mom and my sisters.

Expectations were very high for us to succeed in school and be successful when we left the home. I don't remember ever needing anything that my parents did not provide. Since they hadn't finished high school, they were so proud when we graduated. College was always an option and encouraged.

I am so grateful to my mom for encouraging me to be part of 4-H. I think she saw my leadership abilities as a child, so she encouraged me to participate in all the 4-H activities including speech contests and food demonstrations. I loved competing and winning. I served on many leadership teams for 4-H and school. I even won a trip to the mainland my senior year in high school. My mom and I remodeled a room in the basement. She helped me make a quilt for the bed. My dad helped me make a wardrobe dressing table out of apple boxes. We painted the room together. We submitted our project, and I was selected with twelve others from 4-H from Hawaii to go to Los Angeles, San Francisco, Chicago, Philadelphia, and Washington, DC.

It was November 1963, right after President Kennedy had been killed in Dallas; the Capitol's windows were draped in black. We went to the Arlington National Cemetery, where Kennedy was buried. The flowers were still fresh on his grave. I remember feeling very sad for our country and fearful about the assassination. Coming from a village, I found the large cities overwhelming. I saw my first snow in Chicago; my friends and I ran out of our hotel and onto the streets exclaiming with glee that we were experiencing our first snowfall. I had thought that snow was more like cotton balls, so I was disappointed that it was just small flakes.

Today, Ookala is very desolate; it has just a few homes. The elementary school, store, gas station, and movie theater are gone. In the 1980s, the Ookala Sugar Plantation went out of business, and the village is a very sleepy place with very few people. I give my mom credit for moving out of Ookala before the plantation closed as she wanted us to be near the beach. She convinced my dad to move by going ahead and purchasing land in Waimea. They built a home in five years, which was only twenty minutes from the beach. They built a retirement home that they enjoyed for over twenty years. We loved visiting their home and spending time with them in Waimea. My brothers and sisters and I love sharing our memories of those days.

CHAPTER 9

HER STORY AFFECTS MY STORY

HE REAL STORY OF MY MOM BEGAN BEFORE THE FOUNDATION of the world; God created her in her mother's womb. Was it an accident? For a long time, I thought it was. When someone gets pregnant and it wasn't planned, what do we say? "It was an accident."

It wasn't until after I became a Christian and read the Bible that I realized through (Psalm 139:13–14 NIV), "For it was You who created my inward parts? You knit me together in my mother's womb. I will praise You because I have been remarkably and wonderfully made. Your works are wonderful and I know this very well."

It wasn't an accident that God had created my mom. God knew my mother before she was born. She was knit together in her mother's womb just as I was in my mother's womb. She was not just an illegitimate child forgotten and left behind without a future. God is a sovereign God who knows everything. He created my mom and knew all the circumstances that would surround her life. He knew that she would be placed in the Salvation Army Home for Girls. He knew that her mother would not visit her for years and that she would feel abandoned and not loved by her. He knew the heartache she suffered of waiting for her mother to come and visit and hopefully take her home. He knew that she would be in the home more than ten years before she knew who her mother was.

Her story affected my story. I realized that God is in control of all things and that my mom was not an accident. She was a child created by God; her story is one of redemption from God's point of view. Once I began to see her story from God's providential and sovereign perspective, I was able to assess my disdain for my grandmother.

When attending a conference called Basic Youth Conflicts sometime in the 1970s in Portland, Oregon, I realized that I needed to forgive my grandmother for having abandoned my mom as a child. I had hate in my heart for my grandmother. At the time, I was married and had three children. After much prayer, I decided to call my grandmother. I had not spoken to her in several years. I was really scared to make the call, but I finally did. After a short conversation, I said, "Grandma, I became a Christian and accepted Jesus into my heart, and because of that, I want to say that I forgive you for the lack of love you've shown me and my mother."

She was very quiet. I am sure she was maybe confused and shocked. I was just glad to get those words out of my mouth. Not sure what she said after that, but I hung up and cried. I felt relief because I had asked her to forgive me, and I felt free from the burden of my sin.

I began to put myself in my great-grandfather and grandmother's shoes; because he was a pastor, he may have been embarrassed and ashamed that she had gotten pregnant. I have been a director and later an associate pastor at Greater Portland Bible Church in Portland, Oregon, for over thirty years. If that had been part of my story, what action or decision would I have taken? I would hope that I would try all I could to contact my daughter and at least make an effort to be with her and her child.

I have so many questions about what happened to my grandmother's parents. They will be the first things I will ask my great-grandfather when I see him in heaven: "Did you try to locate my mom as she was your grandchild? Did you care about what happened to her? Did you make an attempt to find out where your daughter had gone to live? If you did know, why didn't you visit her? What really happened when you found out that your daughter was pregnant? Did you cry? Did you pray?" I'm sure my great-grandparents were devasted and heartbroken, but I wish I could fill in the blanks in this story. Looking back, I realize that it was all under God's control.

What would my mom's life have been like if she had not been taken away? What would my life have been like if my mom had been raised in her original home? The Lord revealed himself to her at the Salvation Army home, and she accepted him into her heart when she was five. She studied the scriptures. Based on what she had written in her Bible, she had memorized the Ten Commandments, the Beatitudes, Psalm 23, Psalm 1, Psalm 91, and the titles of the books of the Bible (Old and New Testaments); she was awarded a Bible when she memorized Psalm 91.

She raised us with the godly principles she had learned from the matrons at the home. She learned to forgive, and she would tell us when we expressed our dismay at her being sent to the home, "Vengeance is with the Lord". This was part of the bible verse: "Do not take revenge, my friends, but leave room for God's wrath, for it is written, "It is mine to avenge; I will repay", says the Lord. (Romans 12:19 NIV) I was puzzled by that. She had learned to forgive her mother and accept her for who she was. Why couldn't I forgive her? I found forgiveness a concept hard to accept.

On my journey, I learned that forgiveness does not mean to forget but to accept God's will in a situation. The wrongs people do to others are their responsibility; taking offense at something someone else has done to others is not my responsibility.

Because of my mom's abandonment, I had difficulty at times feeling the effects of those issues in my life. I really desired to let our children express themselves, but it was difficult for me to work through that and know how to be empathetic toward their views and to accept their feelings about issues.

Because of her resilience and her determination to always be forward thinking, I have adopted her ways of thinking and have taught my children to be kind and generous. She always thought of us first in everything.

Through me, her life has influenced my children and grandchildren. I do not take being a family for granted, and I ask the Lord for ways to perpetuate the harmony and unity in my family. Learning to set boundaries in my life has been a process, but it has been beneficial to the ongoing blessings we have experienced in our family. One guideline that has preserved our family is that if there is conflict that needs to be clarified, we let the two individuals work it out themselves. For example, if I have something that I need to work out with someone in our family, I go directly to that person and address him or her with respect and honor without involving others.

I place a high value on unity because of the impact my mom had on my life and my desire to honor the Lord in our family.

CHAPTER 10

MY DADDY

Y DAD, BONIFACIO SORIANO ETRATA (BONCIONG), WAS born in Binalonan, Pangasinan Province, the Philippines, on July 24, 1912. His parents were Claro Valdez Etrata and Narcissa Soriano. His younger sister, whom my dad barely remembers, died when she was only a year old.

His original name was Juanito, given to him at birth. He was told that he had been sick when he was very young and that it was customary to change the name of a sick child so that things would get better for him or her. He was then renamed and blessed as Bonciong. It was a Filipino tradition for a child to be given his or her mother's maiden name, and hers was Soriano. When he arrived in Hawaii to work in the sugar plantation, he decided to accept Bonifacio instead of Bonciong.

He remembers living in Bario Anayao Village. His house was made of wood and napa grass. It was one big room with a big kitchen. He lived on two hectares, about five acres. They grew rice, tobacco, sweet potatoes, and sugarcane. He remembers that his father was fair, skinny, strong, and very well dressed. He had short hair and was a very hardworking man who was wise and smart and a leader in the village. He remembers his mother always preparing food. She was an attractive and nicely dressed woman with short hair, and she was always concerned about her family.

My dad was basically raised by his paternal grandmother because his mom and dad were busy working in the fields. They eventually separated and divorced. He was a couple of villages away from where he was born, and he said he would periodically sneak out to see his mother and father.

He started school when he was six. He went first to a Spanish school and then to an English School, Lumangangan School, till second grade. He then went to Laoha School until the fifth grade. His sixth and seventh grades were spent at the Binalonan School. He then went to Lingan School until he came to Hawaii at age sixteen. He ran track; he liked the 440 and 880 events. He didn't play much with his dad, but he remembered wrestling with him. He also remembered being reprimanded by his dad a lot.

From a young age, he worked in the garden tending the rice patch, tobacco, and sweet potato fields from sunup to sundown. He had the responsibility of caring for the animals. If he lost any, he remembered, he faced punishment and being deprived of meals. He remembered swimming in the gulches.

He wanted to join the Philippine Island Navy, but he didn't pass the test, so he and his best friend, Pedro, quit school and went to Hawaii with Claro. He recalled how scared he was traveling by ship, the *Cleveland*, to Hawaii. My dad and his father were in steerage, the bottom compartment. On the voyage, he learned that he didn't have sailors' legs; for twenty-eight days, he was so sick that he thought he would die. The only things he ate were burnt rice and apples.

He recalled how his father was more afraid than he was because the sailors just threw dead people overboard. My dad lost so much weight on that trip that his fear of boats lasted his whole life. While traveling across the Pacific to Hawaii, he heard stories like eagles and people eating those who came from the Philippines!

The importation of Filipino workers called "Sakadas," which roughly translates to "filipino migrant workers" ... began in 1906 and continued until 1946. During that time an estimated 125,000 Filipinos were recruited from the Illocos and Visayas regions of the Philippines to work in Hawaii. Initially, Filipino men were recruited by the Hawaiian Sugar Planters' Association (HSPA) from the Philippines to Hawaii to work in the sugarcane fields ... Filipino migrant workers were recruited to replace Japanese workers that had been going on strike because of low pay, long work hours and substandard living conditions. These ethnic groups were segregated so that the Filipinos would not be influenced by the striking Japanese workers and so the Filipinos could be used as leverage against the striking Japanese. Filipino workers that lacked education and had previous experience in agricultural work were preferred by recruiters because they were perceived to be easier exploit and control. Sakadas were 3 year contract workers and did not have the intention to stay in Hawaii. Most wanted to make their riches and go back home with enough money to buy land. This was common practice up until the 1940's. The contracts gave them passage to Hawaii and then back to the Philippines after their contract was over. In the 1940's perception of working in Hawaii became glorya (glory) and so more Filipinos sought to stay in Hawaii. Workers were housed in plantation barracks that they paid rent for, worked long 10 hour days, 6 days a week and were paid 90 cents a day. They were the lowest paid workers of all the enthnicities working on the plantations. Most sakadas were single males; however, over time sakadas would send relatives or bring families with them. The last sakadas in 1946 were notable and different compared to all the sakadas prior and are referred to as Sakada "46. Several factors making the Sakada'46 different was that it included more women, children and relatives of previous sakadas. It was also different in that some had an American colonial education, and professionals were included.[1]

---

[1] Wikipedia.org/Filipinos_in_Hawaii.

CHAPTER 11

"I DISOWN YOU"

AFTER MY FATHER AND HIS FATHER HAD BEEN IN HAWAII for three years, his father wanted to return to the Philippines as I had mentioned. When my father, age sixteen, decided to stay because he was enjoying his single life and making money, my grandfather disowned him. In the Filipino culture, refusing to listen to your elders and especially your dad was considered very disrespectful.

I can imagine how sad my grandfather was knowing that he was going back to the Philippines without his only son. I'm not sure how my dad felt, but I assume that by then, he wanted to make a life of his own. Did he suffer rejection? Did he think about what he had done?

My dad said many times about his life in the Philippines, "We had lots of food because we grew rice, sugar, bananas, and vegetables and raised pigs, but we did not have money!" It was a dream for my dad to work, earn money, and have fun with his working mates. He loved playing baseball and was pretty good at it. We were told that many girls liked him. My dad's story was that he met my mom at a party, and according to my mom, he pestered her and kept coming to her table to serve her food.

As a child, I loved going to the parties. Many times, there were long tables of people, and Filipino men served the food. It was very festive and inviting, and the food was delicious!

My dad lived with feelings of rejection and abandonment but never once shared how he felt about his father leaving him. My mom shared that my dad was affected by that but never wanted to talk about it. He never talked about it to us as children, but my impression was that he hoped to someday see his father again. He became involved with his family and became very busy working and providing for it.

In 1977, when my dad was sixty-five, he received the news that his father had died and had left everything to him. It was the Filipino custom for the eldest son to inherit everything. My dad was the only son, but he had assumed that his dad had forgotten him and would leave him nothing; however, his father had left him a lot of land. His father had taken pride in his land; with subsistence living, they were able to exchange and barter with family and friends. They had rice and sugarcane fields and a banana grove.

My mom said that my dad wept when he received the news that his dad had died and had left him everything. He felt guilty for not having made an effort to contact his dad; he had thought this his dad was still angry with him.

In 1977, he went back to the Philippines with my sister, Evelyn, and her husband, Joe Gomera, and reconnected with his family; his mother had longed to see him again. The story was that his mother wept and cried in his arms and didn't want to let him go. What a special reunion. My dad cherished that moment with his mother.

In 2002, my husband, Doug, and I went to the Philippines and saw where my dad had grown up, and we met some relatives. The name Etrata, my surname, was not known in Hawaii. With the help of a very kind woman who worked in city hall in Binalonan and one of my dad's relatives (who looked like my dad when he was younger) took us to meet the family in the village where my dad had grown up. One relative said, "This is your family!"

I hadn't grown up with any cousins on my dad's side, and there were so many. They looked like me and my brothers and sisters. I was overwhelmed. I didn't know how to feel because before we left for the Philippines, my dad was afraid of our visiting the relatives because he was told that they were fighting for his property. But the Lord protected us, and it was a very historical and heartwarming experience.

CHAPTER 12

LEGACY OF MY MOM AND DAD

MY MOM'S AND DAD'S STORIES ARE ABOUT HOW THEY LIVED their lives with God's strength despite having been abandoned and neglected. They knew God would be with them and would give them strength. In Joshua 1:9 NIV, we read, "Have I not commanded you? Be strong and courageous. Do not be afraid; do not be discouraged, for the Lord your God will be with you wherever you go." They had different stories with different issues, but they depended on each other and on the Lord. I don't think they talked about it in the language of abandonment, but I'm sure their emotions of loneliness and having been left behind were similar.

I don't think I acknowledged or recognized their pain. My siblings and I realized as children that we were growing up without real connections with our grandparents. We had aunts and uncles on my mom's side once she connected with them. My aunt Nora, my mom's sister, played a significant part in my life growing up. She made life fun and loved to spend time with us. With a large family, we spent a lot of time playing with one another. Life was simple. Our community of about five hundred people was the extent of our social life.

I watched my mom live her life with the purpose of giving hope to each of her children despite the unbelievable tests and trials she had been through. My mom was an introvert, more of an observer than someone who went out of her way to talk to others, but she was a planner and a forward thinker.

Though my dad worked ten- to twelve-hour days, I never heard him complain about that. I guess he was of the generation that believed that working hard was just part of life. He appreciated being in Hawaii because he could earn money, something that was hard to come by in the Philippines even if food wasn't. He was always willing to do things for us and provide for us. In the culture in which I grew up, fathers were revered, and we served ours in whatever way we could. My mom would make his lunch or dinner, and if he was working, we would take it to him at the mill. He would always give us a treat when we did that.

Being very involved in 4-H, he would take me to competitions in Hilo. Even when he worked the night shift, he would take me and would always say, "You going win!" My dad was my biggest cheerleader when I was involved in anything at school or in the community. He never complained about driving me anywhere I needed to go.

My dad affected my view and experience of my heavenly father. My father was very loving and accepting of me as a person. He was a man of few words, but he demonstrated his love by doing things for his children. He taught us things about whatever he was involved in at the moment whether it was feeding the pigs, going fishing, making cement, or learning to drive.

I praise God for the way my dad showed love to us throughout his life, and he lived to age ninety-six. He wanted us to know that we were loved, and he demonstrated that by the way he treated us—with unconditional love. He had two favorite sayings: "No can help" and "If can can, if no can, no can." These two sayings helped me tell God, "You are sovereign, the blessed controller of all things." He also encouraged us whenever we were involved in a project to do a little bit at a time. He would say, "Little bit, little bit." That taught me to be patient.

He was proud to have seven children because he was the only child and wanted lots of children. He treated us all with love and respect. His early childhood had been stable, and he really looked up to his grandmother because she had taken care of him when his mom and dad went to work.

My mom and dad were wonderful grandparents to our children. They have very fond memories of my parents. We went to visit them in Hawaii every two or three years. They remembered my mom making homemade bread every day when we visited. They remember my dad taking them to get fresh malasadas (a fresh donut that was hot when you ordered them). The malasadas was introduced to the islands by the Portuguese. He also took them to the beach and fishing.

After a few years of working in the mill, my dad was promoted to a supervisor position. This was an honor because Filipinos were hired to do menial work in the fields or work in the mill, not to supervise others. My dad was one of the first Filipinos to become a US citizen. He was so proud of his citizenship, and he loved the flag. He felt privileged to be an American. My dad was a true US patriot.

My dad was promoted because he was very responsible and well liked. Growing up, we heard high praises about my dad. My dad was very ambitious in a very quiet way. He was very collaborative in his style. He would always tell us to have a cool head; that came from Proverbs 15:1 NIV: "A gentle answer turns away wrath."

Because of his promotion, the family moved to Kukui Village, where I was born. The houses there were small, but they were painted. How my parents and we seven children lived in a place with just three bedrooms and one bathroom is truly a miracle! Our home did not feel small because many times, we were outside. Everyone had the same lifestyle with the same number of bedrooms and one bathroom. We shared beds. My sisters each shared beds, and we have so many fond memories of those days. We had a huge vegetable garden and chickens. My favorites were playing under our house, making mud pies, and playing house.

When I was in third grade, my dad had our house built on a hill that overlooked the ocean. It was amazing to see ships and sometimes whales in the ocean. I took that view for granted then, but I love going back to see the home today.

Picture taken in 2012 of my first home in Kukui Village

Picture taken in 2012 of our second home in
Milo Village; Home overlooks the ocean

CHAPTER 13

MY SPIRITUAL JOURNEY BECAME OUR SPIRITUAL JOURNEY

I N FIFTH GRADE, I DECIDED I WANTED TO BECOME A NUN. I WENT to catechism every Tuesday afternoon, and I met some amazing nuns whom I wanted to emulate. I worked hard learning my catechism, and I strove to be as good as I could be because I was a Catholic. I did well in school and knew that I wanted to go to college.

One day when I was in sixth grade, I decided to tell my mom about my desire to become a nun. I prayed at an altar I had created by pulling out a dresser drawer far enough to make a shelf with a cloth over it. I asked God to give me the courage to tell my mom.

So finally, while I was helping my mom in the kitchen, I told her that I wanted to become a nun. Her first response was, "If you do, you won't be able to have children." I hadn't considered that; I told her that I wanted to have children. I was devasted at the thought of never having children; I abandoned the idea of becoming a nun. I was still very devoted to worshipping God, however; when I went to college, I continued going to mass. By the end of my freshman year in college, though, I was attending church less and less and finally stopped going altogether, but I was still devoted to the Catholic Church.

In my freshman year, I met Doug Wachsmuth (my husband now of fifty-three years), and when we decided to marry, I insisted that it had to be in the Catholic Church. I would not marry him until he took catechism classes. We were married at St. John Fisher, a church in Portland, on December 30, 1967, and our reception was at Doug's parents' home located on 2136 SW Sunset Drive.

After we married, I felt a vacuum in my heart for God. I tried going to church, but I still felt empty. Doug was finishing college at Oregon State University, and we lived in Corvallis. I graduated from Pacific University in Forest Grove, Oregon, and I was doing some substitute teaching. I would pass churches and feel very lost and lonely. I decided to read the Bible, but I remembered that I couldn't understand any of it, so I abandoned that idea.

We moved to Newport, Oregon, in 1968 after Doug graduated from Oregon State and began working on the family's oyster farm on Yaquina Bay. Doug's father told him that he was needed there because the manager had had a heart attack. I was so disappointed that we were moving to Newport that I cried as we packed up to move. I had thought that we were going to move to Portland, where Doug would work at a restaurant and I would be doing speech therapy in the Portland School District. But after we moved to the farm, I got a job as a speech therapist for the Lincoln County School District and served students at eight schools.

I ignored the God-shaped vacuum in my heart until one afternoon when Doug and I were shopping for groceries. We were arguing about finances, and I told him, "I don't want to go home with you!"

He asked, "What do you want to do? We have groceries in the car, and we need to go home."

I said, "Let's go to the movies."

So we went to a theater in Newport and saw *The Restless Ones*; I thought, *That's us*. As we watched the movie, I began to feel a tug on my heart because it was a movie about a family that had fallen apart but was brought together through a Billy Graham crusade. I had no idea who Billy Graham was, but the movie was about how much God loved us.

At the end, I started crying. As we were getting ready to leave, a gentleman got up on the stage and announced that those who wanted to talk with someone about what they had experienced were to meet in the back of the theater. I got up and wanted to go, and Doug said that he would go too.

We went to the back of the theater and met an older man, Burl Shoemake. I was crying and scared because being a Catholic, I felt guilty about being influenced by someone outside the Catholic Church. So Doug had to answer the questions that Burl asked, including, "If you knew there was a God, would you want to do what that God told you to do?" Doug said that if he knew there was a God, he would be a fool not to do what that God told him to do. Upon that response, Burl asked if we wanted to meet with him and Bernita, his wife.

We met with them on Wednesday nights for about a year and a half, and they taught us the Bible. They brought projectors and showed us stories about the Bible. We experienced the love of God through Burl and Bernita; we experienced God's love through their many acts of love toward us. They demonstrated through serving us that there was a God who loved us and wanted us to live lives devoted to following Jesus. After a year and half of studying the Bible, Doug and I accepted Jesus Christ as our Savior and were baptized in August 1970, when our son Ted was 3 months old.

Our lives were changed through the work of the Holy Spirit; we have seen God's blessings in our lives for the past fifty-plus years. God had been there for us through all our struggles, through times of great disappointment and loss. He gave us hope and the courage to live worthy of the calling He has given us. I look back now and realize that as I was experiencing the loss of God in my life and the God-shaped vacuum that needed to be filled, He had a plan for me. He truly is the blessed controller of all things in our lives.

CHAPTER 14

THE CHAIN WAS BROKEN

M Y MOM'S AND DAD'S LIVES BEGAN WITH ABANDONMENT, but they lived with hope for the future. They wanted a life together that was better that what they had experienced individually. They went from paradise lost to paradise gained. They were a team who chose to survive and thrive. They did not give up; they lived with hope.

With God's help, my mom and dad broke the chain of despair. Their lives were not free of hardship, sorrow, disappointment, and sometimes hopelessness, but they lived one day at a time. God protected them as they remained married for sixty-six years. My mom died unexpectedly; we had the privilege of having my dad for seven years with him being in each of our homes for a time. He served us in our homes by doing construction projects and gardening, and he always had a positive attitude of love and joy. He would say almost every day, "This is the best day of my life!"

We have now been Christians for over fifty years, and as we reflect on our lives, we feel very grateful and blessed for all God has done for us. We have three beautiful married children: Ted and Stephanie, Keoni and Michelle, and Jon and Beth, and eight amazing grandchildren: Kai, Malia, Hana, Caleb, JD, Chloe, Kaleo, and Kiana. We love them so much and feel so privileged to be parents and grandparents. They bring joy to our life every day!

The Lord has truly blessed our family. We are not free of problems or stresses, but we know to whom we can turn in times of grief, sadness, confusion, and despair for direction and confidence in every aspect of our lives. We want our children and grandchildren to know that God loves them unconditionally and that He died on the cross for them. They can trust Him and lean on Him at all times. He walks with them every day.

At this writing, it has been over a year that the pandemic has been raging. It has been difficult to adjust to all the changes in communication and contact with our family. Communicating with Zoom has been a real asset, but dealing with all the restrictions has been unbearable at times. But we know that God is our only hope (Psalm 33:22). We ask for grace and mercy as we live one day at a time. He is the blessed controller of all things!

Doug and I came into our marriage with brokenness on both sides of our families. Through God's unconditional love, mercy, and grace, we can see how He truly has broken the chain of bondage that has been passed down through the generations. We can achieve victory because Jesus Christ died on the cross for all our sins past and present. What a comfort to know we have a God who accepts us just as we are. He pursues us every day with His love. His Word is living and gives life to us every day! This is our prayer for our family:

The Lord bless you and protect you. The Lord makes His face shine upon you and be gracious to you. The Lord looks upon you with favor and gives you peace. (Numbers 6:24–26NIV)

This verse sums up our lives today.

> For the Lord is good. His love is endures forever; his faithfulness endures through all generations. (Psalm 100:5 NIV)

Taken with my husband and children in 2012
at the Kalemela Church in Paauhau

Etrata extended family reunion of 2012

2012 Hawaii vacation with the family

50th Wedding Anniversary Celebration
with the grandkids (and parents)

APPENDIX

Charles Kamakawiwo'ole, Preacher

REVEREND CHARLES MOSES KAMAKAWIWO'OLE

MARCH 21, 1850 TO MARCH 6, 1931

KALEMELA EAST HAMAKUA PROTESTANT CHURCH, PA'AUHAU MAUKA, WAS FIRST ESTABLISHED IN 1859-1860. REVEREND KAMAKAWIWO'OLE WAS A YOUNG PRACTICING MINISTER AT KALEMELA WHEN HE RECEIVED A PETITION ON APRIL 22, 1888 FROM THE CHURCH MEMBERS TO BE THEIR MINISTER. REVEREND KAMAKAWIWO'OLE WAS CROWNED AS PASTOR OF KALEMELA CHURCH, PA'AUHAU MAUKA ON SEPTEMBER 9, 1888.

Placard of Charles Kamakawiwo'ole

Kalemela Church Exterior

Kalemela Church Interior, My husband
Doug and me in the background

Etrata Genealogy

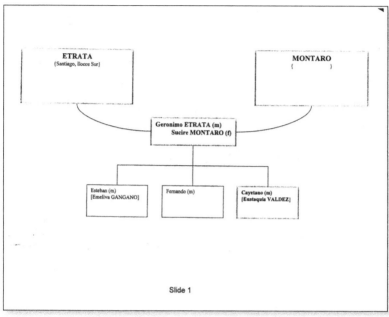

Slide 1

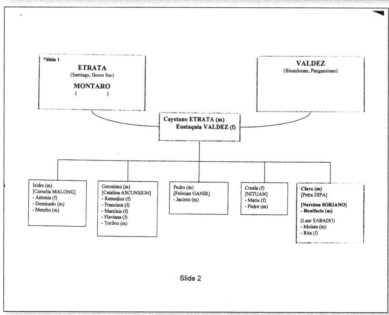

Slide 2

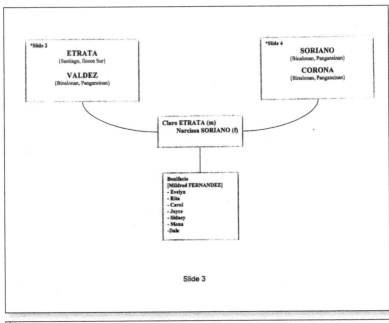

Slide 3

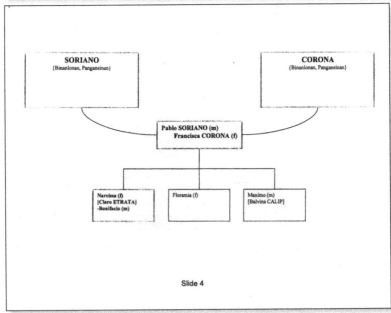

Slide 4

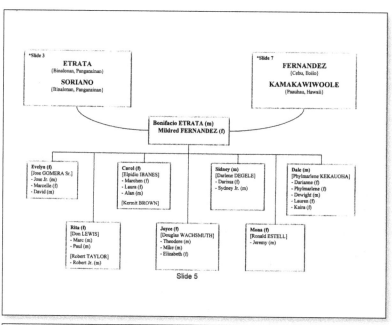

Slide 5

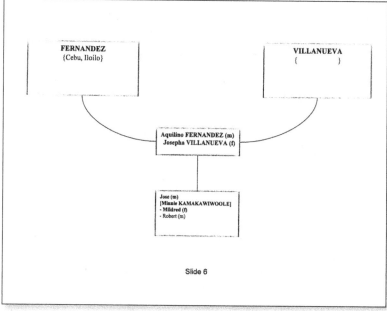

Slide 6

Kamakawiwo'ole Genealogy

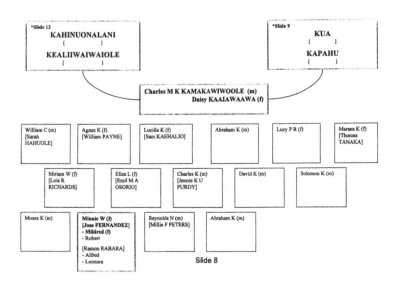

Slide 13
KAHINUONALANI
(   )
KEALIIWAIWAIOLE
(   )

Slide 9
KUA
(   )
KAPAHU
(   )

Charles M K KAMAKAWIWOOLE (m)
Daisy KAAIAWAAWA (f)

| William C (m) [Sarah HAHUOLE] | Agnes K (f) [William PAYNE] | Lucilla K (f) [Sam KAEHALIO] | Abraham K (m) | Lucy P R (f) | Marnea K (f) [Thomas TANAKA] |

| Miriam W (f) [Lois R RICHARDS] | Eliza L (f) [Emil M A OSORIO] | Charles K (m) [Jennie K U PURDY] | David K (m) | Solomon K (m) |

Moses K (m)

Minnie W (f)
[Jose FERNANDEZ]
- Mildred (f)
- Robert

[Ramon RABARA]
- Alfred
- Leonora

Reynolds N (m)
[Millie F PETERS]

Abraham K (m)

Slide 8

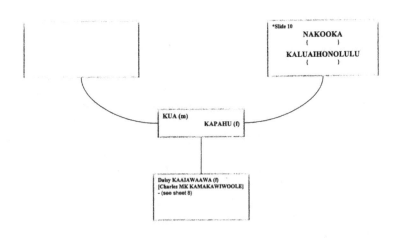

Slide 10
NAKOOKA
(   )
KALUAIHONOLULU
(   )

KUA (m)
KAPAHU (f)

Daisy KAAIAWAAWA (f)
[Charles MK KAMAKAWIWOOLE]
- (see sheet 8)

Side 9